HOCKEY HALL OF FAME

DOMINANT DEFENSEMEN

HOCKEY HALL OF FAME

DOMINANT DEFENSEMEN

ERIC ZWEIG

ILLUSTRATIONS BY
GEORGE TODOROVIC

FIREFLY BOOKS

A FIREFLY BOOK

Published by Firefly Books Ltd. 2014

First printing

Publisher Cataloging-in-Publication Data (U.S.)
A CIP record for this title is available from the Library of Congress

Library and Archives Canada Cataloguing in Publication
A CIP record for this title is available from Library and Archives Canada

Published in the United States by
Firefly Books (U.S.) Inc.
P.O. Box 1338, Ellicott Station
Buffalo, New York 14205

Published in Canada by
Firefly Books Ltd.
50 Staples Avenue, Unit 1
Richmond Hill, Ontario L4B 0A7

Cover and interior design: Kimberley Young
Illustrations: George Todorovic
Creative Direction: Steve Cameron

Printed in China

The publisher gratefully acknowledges the financial support for our publishing program
by the Government of Canada through the Canada Book Fund as administered by
the Department of Canadian Heritage.

CONTENTS

PLUS

MIKE GREEN, MARC STAAL,
SHEA WEBER, ZDENO CHARA,
DUNCAN KEITH, KRIS LETANG,
DION PHANEUF, P.K. SUBBAN,
DREW DOUGHTY, ERIK KARLSSON,
RYAN SUTER AND MANY MORE!

BOBBY ORR

Hockey Hall of Fame: 1979

MOST EXPERTS CONSIDER BOBBY ORR TO BE THE GREATEST DEFENSEMAN TO EVER PLAY. MANY EVEN THINK HE WAS THE GREATEST PLAYER OF ALL-TIME! BEFORE BOBBY ORR, THERE HAD BEEN OFFENSIVE-MINDED DEFENSEMEN, BUT NO ONE HAD PLAYED THE WAY ORR DID. HIS SPEEDY SKATING, CREATIVE PASSING AND

MIKE GRANT (HHOF: 1950)

Blast FROM THE Past

Mike Grant may have been hockey's first offensive defenseman. Grant played with the Montreal Victorias in the 1890s! He'd been a champion speed skater as a boy and brought that skill to hockey. After joining the Victorias for the 1893–94 season, Grant's speed on the ice helped turn his team into champions. The Vics won the Stanley Cup from 1895 to 1899, and his rushing style influenced his teammates. In a Stanley Cup game in 1899, Grant's defense partner Graham Drinkwater rushed the puck from end to end in the final seconds to score the winning goal.

his awesome offensive skills changed the way hockey was played forever. Very soon, every team was looking to add their own Bobby Orr.

NHL scouts first noticed Orr when he was only 12 years old. By the time he was 18, he had joined the Boston Bruins in the NHL. Orr was easily the most exciting new player of 1966–67, and his unique style won him the Calder Trophy as the NHL rookie of the year. The next year, he won the Norris Trophy as the NHL's best defenseman. He won that award eight years in a row!

Orr set a record for defensemen when he scored 21 goals in 1968–69, then he smashed it with 33 goals in 1969–70. That year, he recorded 120 points, which made Orr the first defenseman ever to top 100 points and the first defenseman to lead the entire league in scoring. He is still the only defenseman in NHL history to win the scoring title, and he did it twice! Orr

was no slouch on defense either. He wasn't a big hitter, but his skating and positioning was so strong that offensive players rarely got around him.

Orr scored the winning goal in overtime to give Boston the Stanley Cup in 1970 and he helped them win it again in 1972. Sadly, Orr suffered a series of serious knee injuries that forced him to retire when he was only 30 years old. He barely played nine full seasons in the NHL.

Did You Know?

BOBBY ORR WAS THE FIRST PLAYER TO WIN THE HART TROPHY AS NHL MVP THREE YEARS IN A ROW. FROM 1969–70 TO 1971–72.

THE NORRIS TROPHY

The NHL's annual award for best defenseman is officially known as the James Norris Memorial Trophy. Most people call it the Norris Trophy. But who was James Norris? Norris grew up in Montreal and later became a wealthy businessman in Chicago. In 1932, he bought the NHL team in Detroit and changed its name from Falcons to Red Wings. When James Norris died in 1952, his children wanted to do something special to honor him. Before the start of the 1953–54 season, they donated a trophy in his name. Five-time winner Raymond Bourque can be seen holding the trophy at right.

NORRIS TROPHY: 1987, 1988, 1990, 1991, 1994

Raymond BOURQUE

PAUL COFFEY

HOCKEY HALL OF FAME: 2004

PAUL COFFEY MAY BE THE SMOOTHEST SKATER IN NHL HISTORY. HE WAS SUPER FAST, BUT HIS MOVEMENTS SEEMED EFFORTLESS. "WHEN HE WANTS TO," HIS TEAMMATE WAYNE GRETZKY ONCE SAID, "HE CAN GO AROUND ANYONE IN THE LEAGUE. HE DOESN'T EVEN HAVE TO STRIDE AROUND THEM. HE GETS GOING SO FAST, HE JUST GLIDES BY."

KING CLANCY (HHOF: 1958)

Blast FROM THE Past

King Clancy began his NHL career with the Ottawa Senators in 1921–22. Ottawa was one of the best teams in hockey at the time and Clancy helped them win the Stanley Cup in 1923 and 1927. At 5-foot-7 (170 cm) and only 155 pounds (70 kg) Clancy was small for an NHL defenseman, but he never backed down from bigger opponents. Like Coffey, he was one of the top-scoring defensemen of his day. Before the 1930–31 season, Clancy was traded to Toronto for $35,000 and two players. At the time, it was the most expensive trade in hockey history!

The Edmonton Oilers chose Coffey sixth overall in the 1980 NHL Draft. Many teams like to leave their young defensemen in junior hockey or the minors to gain experience. Not the Oilers! They were a young team on the rise and they wanted all their top stars working together right away in the NHL. Coffey's numbers were nothing special as a rookie in 1980–81, but by the 1981–82 season, he and the Oilers were ready to take off. Coffey's quick skating made him a perfect fit with Gretzky and the high-flying offense in Edmonton. By the 1983–84 season, the Oilers were Stanley Cup champions and Coffey had joined Bobby Orr as the only defensemen in NHL history to score 40 goals in a single season. In 1985–86, Coffey almost became the first defenseman to score 50! He fell just short with 48, though he did break Orr's record of 46. Coffey's career-high 138 points that season were just one behind Orr's record total of 139. Before the 1987–88 season, Edmonton traded Coffey to Pittsburgh where he got to team up with another superstar, Mario Lemieux.

Great as he was as a goal scorer, Coffey was even more dangerous setting up his teammates. He was often among the league's leaders in assists and was the first defenseman in NHL history to top 1,000 in his career. Coffey's lifetime total of 1,135 assists ranks him fifth among all players in NHL history.

Did You Know?

PAUL COFFEY WON THREE STANLEY CUPS WITH EDMONTON AND ONE WITH PITTSBURGH. HE ALSO WON THE NORRIS TROPHY TWICE WITH EDMONTON AND ONCE WITH DETROIT.

MIKE GREEN OF the Washington Capitals broke out as the best offensive defenseman in the NHL between 2007 and 2010. Though injuries have slowed him down since then, he is still a tremendous skater with a powerful slap shot. At his best, he often plays like a fourth forward on the ice. In 2008–09, Green scored 31 times to become the first defenseman in 16 years to reach the 30-goal plateau. Between January 27 and February 14, 2009, Green set a modern record for NHL defensemen by scoring a goal in eight straight games!

MODERN MATCH
MIKE GREEN

BRIAN LEETCH

Hockey Hall of Fame: 2009

BRIAN LEETCH IS THE ONLY MEMBER OF THE HOCKEY HALL OF FAME BORN IN TEXAS. HIS FAMILY LEFT THE LONE STAR STATE WHEN HE WAS A BABY, AND HE GREW UP IN THE TOWN OF CHESHIRE, CONNECTICUT, WHERE HIS FATHER MANAGED THE TOWN RINK. BY THE TIME HE WAS A TEENAGER, LEETCH WAS A STAR IN TWO ▎▎▎➤

CHOSEN 12TH OVERALL in the 2005 NHL Draft, Marc Staal was only the third defenseman to be selected by the Rangers in the first round of the draft since they chose Brian Leetch back in 1986. Marc is one of four Staal brothers to play in the NHL. Oldest brother Eric is a top scorer with the Carolina Hurricanes, while Jordan is a talented two-way center, also with the Hurricanes. Youngest brother Jared has yet to play full-time in the big leagues. Marc is the only defenseman among the Staal brothers. He's a hard checker, but also a strong skater with good offensive instincts.

MODERN MATCH
MARC STAAL

different sports. In Grade 10, he earned All-State honors in hockey while pitching his local high school baseball team to the state championship. After his senior year at the prestigious Avon Old Farms prep school, Leetch was chosen ninth overall by the New York Rangers in the 1986 NHL Draft.

Leetch didn't join the Rangers right away. In 1986–87, he attended Boston College where his father had also played hockey. The next year, Leetch joined the United States national team and played at the 1988 Calgary Olympics. He joined the Rangers after the Winter Games and picked up an assist in his first NHL contest! Leetch was a strong skater with fantastic offensive instincts. In his first full season with the Rangers in 1988–89, he won the Calder Trophy after scoring 23 goals. That's a rookie record for NHL defensemen that still stands!

During the next few years, Leetch helped the Rangers grow into champions. In 1991–92, he established career highs with 80 assists and 102 points, joining Bobby Orr, Denis Potvin, Paul Coffey and Al MacInnis as one of only five defensemen in NHL history to top 100 points in a season. Leetch won the Norris Trophy that season, and again in 1996–97. In 1993–94, the Rangers won the Stanley Cup for the first time in 54 years. When they did, Leetch became the first American-born player to win the Conn Smythe Trophy as playoff MVP!

BATTERED BLADES

Brian Leetch wore these skates while starring with the Rangers from 1989 to 1995. They show plenty of wear and tear from six seasons in the NHL. In all, Leetch played 18 seasons in the league before retiring in 2006. He spent 16-plus seasons with the Rangers and holds the franchise record with 741 assists. Leetch was traded to Toronto late in the 2003–04 season. After a lockout wiped out the 2004–05 campaign, he returned to play one final season in the NHL as a member of the Boston Bruins.

FROM THE VAULT

DENIS POTVIN

Hockey Hall of Fame: 1991

Bobby Orr was still going strong when Denis Potvin entered the NHL in 1973–74. Soon, injuries would end Orr's career and Potvin became the NHL's best blueliner. That made sense, since Potvin had been the most hyped defenseman to come out of junior hockey since Bobby Orr. ▶

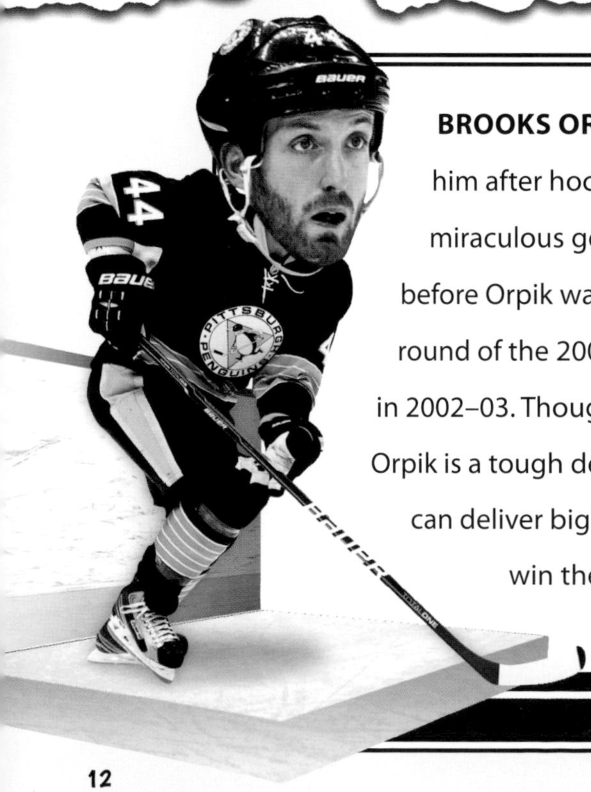

BROOKS ORPIK WAS destined to be a hockey player. His parents named him after hockey coach Herb Brooks, who led the United States to a miraculous gold medal victory at the 1980 Winter Olympics a few months before Orpik was born. The Pittsburgh Penguins chose Orpik in the first round of the 2000 NHL Draft and he became a regular with the team in 2002–03. Though he doesn't have Denis Potvin's offensive skill, Orpik is a tough defenseman who blocks shots and can deliver big hits. He helped the Penguins win the Stanley Cup in 2009.

MODERN MATCH
BROOKS ORPIK

Like Orr, Potvin began his junior career when he was only 14 years old. During the early 1970s, a player had to be 20 years old to enter the NHL, not 18. That meant Potvin spent five full seasons playing junior hockey. In his final Ontario Hockey League season of 1972–73, Potvin shattered Orr's defenseman record of 94 points by collecting 123 points! The New York Islanders were the worst team in the NHL that season, which gave them the top choice in the 1973 Draft. To no one's surprise, they picked Potvin.

Did You Know?

DENIS POTVIN WON THE NORRIS TROPHY THREE TIMES IN HIS CAREER AND FINISHED SECOND IN VOTING TWICE.

Potvin's older brother Jean played with the Islanders too, and that made it easier for Denis to break into the NHL. He won the Calder Trophy as rookie of the year and soon helped make the Islanders one of the league's best teams. When Potvin was named team captain in 1979–80, he led the Islanders to their first of four straight Stanley Cup wins!

Potvin was strong and sturdy on the ice. He was a tough player who delivered hard hits, but he was just as dangerous in the other team's zone. In 1978–79, Potvin joined Orr as the second defenseman to score 100 points in a season. Potvin was the first defenseman in NHL history to score 300 career goals and also the first to reach 1,000 points. He topped 30 goals on three occasions and had six other seasons with 20 goals or more.

Blast FROM THE Past — HARVEY PULFORD (HHOF: 1945)

There has been a long tradition of hockey excellence in Ottawa, Ontario. In the early 1900s, the Ottawa "Silver Seven" were the game's best team and Harvey Pulford was the team's best defenseman. Pulford played many sports, including lacrosse, football and rowing. In hockey, he was a hardnosed defenseman, who, like Denis Potvin, was unafraid to deliver a punishing check in order to take care of business in his own end. Pulford starred for Ottawa from 1893 to 1908 and helped his team win the Stanley Cup in 1903, 1904, 1905 and 1906!

AL MacINNIS

HOCKEY HALL OF FAME: 2007

AL MacINNIS HAD A BIG SHOT. HE GREW UP IN A FISHING VILLAGE IN NOVA SCOTIA, WHERE HIS FATHER RAN THE LOCAL HOCKEY RINK. MacINNIS USED TO HANG AROUND, COLLECTING PUCKS THAT WENT OVER THE BOARDS. IN SUMMER, HE SPENT HOURS SHOOTING THOSE PUCKS AGAINST HIS FATHER'S BARN. LITTLE DID HE KNOW HE WAS PERFECTING

Powerful Pairs

CHRIS PRONGER

For nine seasons, from 1995–96 through 2003–04, the St. Louis Blues boasted two of the NHL's best defensemen. Joining Al MacInnis on the blue line was a blond-haired giant named Chris Pronger. Standing 6-foot-6 (198 cm) and weighing 220 pounds (99 kg), Pronger loved to use his big body to deliver punishing checks. He was also among the NHL's top-scoring defensemen. In 1999–2000, Pronger became the first defenseman since Bobby Orr back in 1971–72 to be named the best defenseman in the league *and* the league MVP in the same season!

one of the greatest slap shots in hockey history!

The Calgary Flames chose MacInnis in the first round of the 1981 NHL Draft. The team knew they had something special, but they didn't rush him. MacInnis spent most of the next two years playing junior hockey with the Kitchener Rangers. In 1982–83, he was named the best defenseman in the Ontario Hockey League. When he finally made it to Calgary for good midway through the 1983–84 season, MacInnis was ready. Soon, the Flames were one of the best teams in the NHL and MacInnis was one of the league's top defensemen.

MacInnis was solid in front of his own net, but it was his blistering slap shot that had people's attention, especially the terrified goalies on opposing teams! When Calgary won the Stanley Cup in 1989, MacInnis

Did You Know?

USING AN OLD-FASHIONED WOODEN STICK, AL MACINNIS WON THE HARDEST SHOT COMPETITION AT THE NHL ALL-STAR GAME SEVEN TIMES.

led all playoff performers in scoring. He was the first defenseman to do that in 11 years, and he became just the fourth defenseman in NHL history to win the Conn Smythe Trophy as playoff MVP. During the 1990–91 season, MacInnis joined Bobby Orr, Denis Potvin and Paul Coffey as the fourth defenseman in NHL history to top 100 points in a single season! After 13 years in Calgary, MacInnis was traded to St. Louis in 1994. He played 10 more years with the Blues and won the Norris Trophy with them in 1998–99.

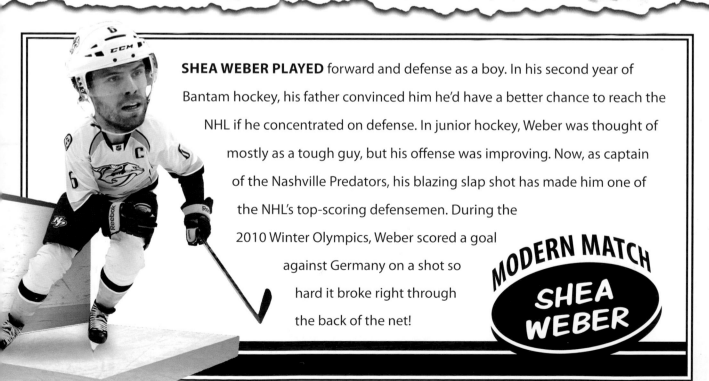

SHEA WEBER PLAYED forward and defense as a boy. In his second year of Bantam hockey, his father convinced him he'd have a better chance to reach the NHL if he concentrated on defense. In junior hockey, Weber was thought of mostly as a tough guy, but his offense was improving. Now, as captain of the Nashville Predators, his blazing slap shot has made him one of the NHL's top-scoring defensemen. During the 2010 Winter Olympics, Weber scored a goal against Germany on a shot so hard it broke right through the back of the net!

MODERN MATCH

SHEA WEBER

EDDIE SHORE

Hockey Hall of Fame: 1947

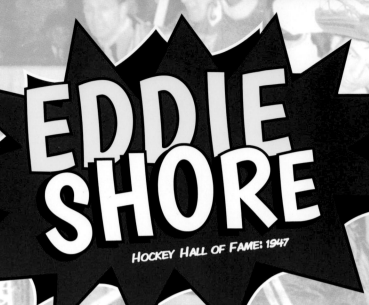

LONG BEFORE BOBBY ORR WOWED NHL FANS IN BOSTON, EDDIE SHORE HAD BEEN THE BEST DEFENSEMAN IN BRUINS HISTORY. IN FACT, MANY CONSIDERED SHORE TO BE THE BEST PLAYER IN THE GAME.

SHORE GREW UP ON A RANCH IN SOUTHERN SASKATCHEWAN. HE DIDN'T PLAY MUCH HOCKEY AS A BOY, BUT ▐▐▐▶

AT 6-FOOT-9 (206 cm), Zdeno Chara is the tallest player in NHL history! He broke into the NHL with the New York Islanders in 1997–98 and later became a star with Ottawa. Since signing with Boston in 2006–07, Chara has gotten even better. He won the Norris Trophy for the first time in 2008–09 and captained Boston to the Stanley Cup in 2011. Chara won the hardest shot competition at the NHL All-Star Game five times in a row between 2007 and 2012. His slap shot has regularly been clocked at over 100 miles per hour (160 kph)!

MODERN MATCH
ZDENO CHARA

his years of hard work with the horses on the ranch made him tough and strong. "It helped me build the [body] I needed to be to play nineteen years of professional hockey," Shore once said. When he joined Boston in 1926–27, the Bruins were in just their third season in the NHL. They'd struggled during their first two years, but Shore helped turn them into the best team in the league. The Bruins won the Stanley Cup for the first time in 1929, and Shore was still starring with the team when they won it again in 1939. He also led the Bruins to the best record in the regular season six times!

Shore skated with long strides that carried him up the ice with blazing speed. His strength made it hard to knock him off the puck, and his nasty temper meant opponents had to pay the price if they did. Shore usually ranked among the top-scoring defensemen in the NHL each season, but he was always high among the penalty leaders too. Still, he was clearly the best defenseman in the league. There was no Norris Trophy when Shore played, but when the NHL began naming its year-end All-Star Teams in 1930–31, Shore was named to the First Team seven times in nine years. He's also the only defenseman in NHL history to win the Hart Trophy as league MVP four times.

Did You Know?

SINCE 1959, THE OUTSTANDING DEFENSEMAN IN THE AMERICAN HOCKEY LEAGUE HAS RECEIVED THE EDDIE SHORE PLAQUE.

SHORE'S LEATHER LID

Eddie Shore's legendary temper once put him in the middle of one of hockey's darkest moments. During a rough game between the Bruins and the Maple Leafs on December 12, 1933, Shore hit Toronto's Ace Bailey from behind. Bailey fell on his head and fractured his skull. For a while, it seemed that Bailey might die from his injuries. He eventually recovered, but never played hockey again. Almost nobody in hockey wore helmets then, but after the Bailey incident, several Boston players began to do so. Eddie Shore wore this leather helmet during the mid-1930s.

FROM THE VAULT

SCOTT NIEDERMAYER

Hockey Hall of Fame: 2013

No player in hockey history has won more different major championships than Scott Niedermayer. His first big victory came with Team Canada at the 1991 World Junior Championship. The next year, he helped his own junior team — the Kamloops Blazers — win the Memorial Cup as the best team in Canadian junior hockey. ▮▮▶

Blast FROM THE Past

CYCLONE TAYLOR (HHOF: 1947)

Cyclone Taylor never played in the NHL, but he's still one of the biggest stars in hockey history. Taylor became famous as a defenseman with the Ottawa Senators in 1907. His real name was Fred, but people called him Cyclone because of his whirlwind speed. He loved to rush the puck, but was always fast enough to get back and help his goalie. Taylor played forward and the old-time position of rover when he joined the Vancouver Millionaires of the Pacific Coast Hockey Association (PCHA) in 1912. There he won five PCHA scoring titles!

Niedermayer later won the Stanley Cup four times during his 18-year NHL career. In 2004 he helped Canada win gold twice — once at the World Championships and again at the World Cup of Hockey! He also earned Olympic gold medals in 2002 and 2010.

Niedermayer was born in Edmonton, Alberta but grew up in Cranbrook, British Columbia. In addition to playing hockey as a boy, he took figure skating lessons when he was seven. Those lessons taught him balance and helped him develop the strong stride that made him one of the fastest skaters in the NHL. In fact, Niedermayer was so smooth on his skates that he sometimes made the game look too easy. Early in his career, people wondered if the slick-skating Niedermayer was willing to compete hard enough to become an NHL star. He quickly proved to be a great team player and a hard worker.

Niedermayer became a regular with the New Jersey Devils in 1992–93. Soon, with goalie Martin Brodeur and fellow defenseman Scott Stevens, the Devils became one of the best teams in the NHL. Niedermayer won the Stanley Cup with New Jersey in 1995, 2000 and 2003. He also won the Norris Trophy in 2003–04. Niedermayer joined the Anaheim Ducks in 2005–06. The Devils beat the Ducks for the Stanley Cup in 2003, but with Niedermayer as their captain, Anaheim won the Stanley Cup in 2007. Niedermayer earned the Conn Smythe Trophy as playoff MVP.

Did You Know?

SCOTT NIEDERMAYER WON THE STANLEY CUP PLAYING AGAINST HIS BROTHER ROB'S TEAM IN 2003 AND THEN WON IT WITH HIM WHEN THEY PLAYED TOGETHER IN 2007.

MODERN MATCH
DUNCAN KEITH

HE MAY NOT skate like Scott Niedermayer, but Duncan Keith of the Chicago Blackhawks is also a strong two-way defenseman. He's known for his offensive skill and his shutdown abilities. Keith started as a forward in minor hockey in Ontario, but was switched to defense and later moved to British Columbia, where he played junior hockey. Keith joined the Blackhawks in 2005–06 and has won the Stanley Cup with Chicago in 2010 and 2013. In 2010, he was also a teammate of Scott Niedermayer when Team Canada won the Olympic gold. Keith won his second Olympic gold medal in 2014.

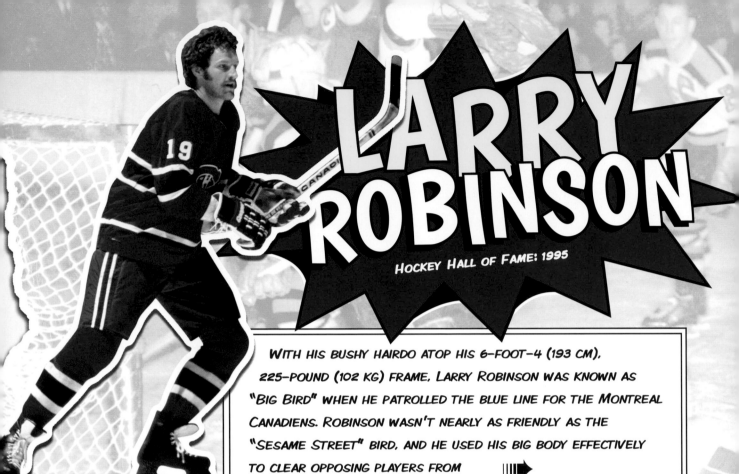

LARRY ROBINSON

HOCKEY HALL OF FAME: 1995

WITH HIS BUSHY HAIRDO ATOP HIS 6-FOOT-4 (193 CM), 225-POUND (102 KG) FRAME, LARRY ROBINSON WAS KNOWN AS "BIG BIRD" WHEN HE PATROLLED THE BLUE LINE FOR THE MONTREAL CANADIENS. ROBINSON WASN'T NEARLY AS FRIENDLY AS THE "SESAME STREET" BIRD, AND HE USED HIS BIG BODY EFFECTIVELY TO CLEAR OPPOSING PLAYERS FROM ▐▐▐▶

Powerful Pairs

SERGE SAVARD (HHOF: 1986)	GUY LAPOINTE (HHOF: 1993)

During the 1970s, Larry Robinson was part of a defensive unit in Montreal known as "The Big Three." The other two players were Serge Savard and Guy Lapointe. Savard, a veteran who became famous for the "spinorama," had plenty of offensive skill, but he developed a stay-at-home style that let Robinson take more chances. Lapointe may have had the most offensive talent of The Big Three. Picking his spots to pinch in and aid the attack, Lapointe topped 20 goals three different times.

the front of his net. His big, booming slap shot also made him dangerous in the offensive zone.

Robinson didn't play defense until he got to junior hockey, and he only did then because his team didn't have enough defensemen. When the Canadiens drafted him in 1971, they decided to keep Robinson at his new position, and sent him to the minors to get more experience. He got his first shot with Montreal in 1972–73, and he took a regular shift with the Canadiens for the rest of the season. Montreal decided not to play him at the start of the playoffs that year, but he worked his way back in and helped the team win the Stanley Cup. Later Robinson helped Montreal win the Cup four years in a row! He also won the Norris Trophy twice, and was named the MVP of the playoffs in 1978. Arguably, the Canadiens

Did You Know?

LARRY ROBINSON WAS THE FIRST NHL PLAYER TO PLAY 200 PLAYOFF GAMES AND NOW RANKS SEVENTH ALL-TIME WITH 227 PLAYOFF GAMES.

of the late 1970s were the greatest team in hockey history. Even so, Robinson's best season in Montreal may have been in 1985–86, when the Canadiens were much weaker. That year he had 19 goals and 63 assists for a career-high 82 points, and Montreal was a surprise winner of the Stanley Cup. It was Robinson's sixth NHL championship! Robinson spent 17 seasons in Montreal and three in Los Angeles. Later, as a coach with New Jersey, he won the Stanley Cup three more times.

KRIS LETANG IS a solid checker, but he doesn't have the size to play the same physical style as Larry Robinson. Still, this native of Montreal is one of the most exciting defensemen in the NHL today. Letang is a silky smooth skater who can move quickly from side to side or burst ahead to lead the attack. Letang spent his first full season in the NHL with Pittsburgh in 2007–08 and was chosen as the team's top rookie.

A year later, in 2008–09, Letang helped the Penguins win the Stanley Cup.

MODERN MATCH

KRIS LETANG

TIM HORTON

HOCKEY HALL OF FAME: 1977

TODAY, HIS NAME MAKES PEOPLE THINK OF COFFEE, DONUTS, SOUP AND SANDWICHES. BUT LONG BEFORE HE WAS KNOWN AS THE NAMESAKE OF ONE OF CANADA'S MOST POPULAR CHAIN RESTAURANTS, TIM HORTON WAS KNOWN AS ONE OF HOCKEY'S BEST DEFENSEMEN. HORTON WAS BORN IN THE NORTHERN ONTARIO TOWN OF ▐▐▐▶

MODERN MATCH
DION PHANEUF

DION PHANEUF IS a tough, two-way defenseman who can deliver punishing body checks while also putting pucks in the net with his powerful shot. Phaneuf grew up in Edmonton, Alberta and played junior hockey in Red Deer. When he began his NHL career in Calgary in 2005–06, Phaneuf became just the third defenseman in league history to score 20 goals in his rookie season. He also finished third in voting for Rookie of the Year behind Alex Ovechkin and Sidney Crosby. Phaneuf was traded to Toronto on January 31, 2010, and was named captain at the start of the 2010–11 season.

Cochrane and later played hockey around nearby Timmins. His real name was Miles Gilbert Horton, but his mother always called him Tim. By the time he was 17, Horton had attracted the attention of the Toronto Maple Leafs. They arranged for him to go to St. Michael's College in Toronto so he could attend school and play hockey. Horton turned pro with the Maple Leafs in 1949, but he wasn't a full-time member of the club until 1952–53. A badly broken leg suffered late in the 1954–55 season slowed him down for the next few years, but by the early 1960s, the Maple Leafs were the best team in hockey and Horton was their best defenseman. With Horton on the blue line, Toronto won the Stanley Cup in 1962, 1963, 1964 and 1967! Coach Punch Imlach would later say that the tough defenseman was more important to those Cup-winning teams than any other player.

Horton was known as the strongest man in the NHL. He could deliver crushing body checks, but he usually used his incredible strength to stop fights, rather than start them. When trouble began, Horton would restrain a player in a powerful grip that became known as the "Horton Bear Hug." His talent and strength kept people in line, and his smooth skating made him an effective player at both ends of the ice. Sadly, Tim Horton was killed in a car accident in 1974 while playing for the Buffalo Sabres.

Did You Know?

TIM HORTON OPENED HIS FIRST RESTAURANT IN HAMILTON, ONTARIO, IN 1964. TODAY, THERE ARE MORE THAN 3,000 TIM HORTONS ACROSS CANADA.

Blast FROM THE Past

HAP DAY (HHOF: 1961)

Clarence Day was so cheerful his friends called him "Happy." Soon, that was shortened to "Hap," and the nickname stuck. Hap Day was originally a defenseman, but when he started in the NHL with the Toronto St. Pats in 1924 they played him at left wing. By the time the team became the Maple Leafs in 1926–27, Day was back on defense. He was a natural-born leader who served as team captain from 1927–28 to 1936–37. Day won the Stanley Cup as a player in 1932 and later coached the Maple Leafs to five more championships in the 1940s!

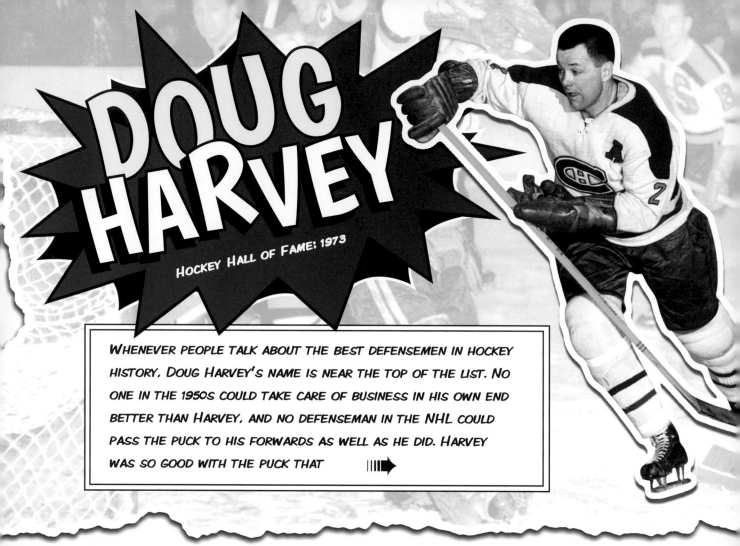

DOUG HARVEY

Hockey Hall of Fame: 1973

Whenever people talk about the best defensemen in hockey history, Doug Harvey's name is near the top of the list. No one in the 1950s could take care of business in his own end better than Harvey, and no defenseman in the NHL could pass the puck to his forwards as well as he did. Harvey was so good with the puck that ▐▐▐▐▶

FROM THE VAULT

LAST HURRAH

Doug Harvey's NHL career seemed to be over when the New York Rangers decided he was too old for them during the 1963–64 season. He played in the minor leagues for the next few years and when the St. Louis Blues joined the NHL as a new expansion team in 1967–68, they signed Harvey as a player-coach for their farm team. Harvey was called up to the NHL when St. Louis made the playoffs, and he helped the Blues reach the Stanley Cup final. He wore this jersey for the Blues against his old team, the Montreal Canadiens.

he controlled the way everyone on the ice played. When he slowed down to survey the situation and look for an opening, everyone else slowed down too. When he sped up again, every player on the ice moved faster. Harvey was the best defenseman on the best team in the NHL, helping the Montreal Canadiens win the Stanley Cup in 1953 and for a record five years in a row from 1956 to 1960!

Great as he was at hockey, Harvey also starred at football and baseball. He was so good at baseball that the Boston Braves of the National League invited him to spring training in 1950. Harvey couldn't go though, as he was a little busy playing in the NHL playoffs with Montreal at the time!

Harvey joined the Canadiens in 1947–48. It took him a little while to adjust to the NHL, but by 1951–52 he was a First-Team

Did You Know?

AMONG DEFENSEMEN, ONLY RAYMOND BOURQUE (19) AND NICKLAS LIDSTROM (12) HAVE BEEN SELECTED AS NHL ALL-STARS MORE TIMES THAN DOUG HARVEY.

All-Star. Harvey was an All-Star for 11 straight seasons, including 10 selections to the First Team. When the NHL began awarding the Norris Trophy in 1954, Harvey won it six times in the first eight years! He won it for a seventh time in 1961–62. He was a member of the New York Rangers that season, serving as a star player and as the team's head coach! In all, Harvey played 20 NHL seasons and retired in 1969 at the age of 44.

MODERN MATCH — P.K. SUBBAN

SIX DIFFERENT DEFENSEMEN have won the Norris Trophy while playing for the Montreal Canadiens, more than any other team in the NHL. The most recent member of this record-setting club is Pernell Karl Subban. Better known as P.K. Subban, he won the Norris Trophy in 2012–13. Subban is a great skater with a hard shot. He can lead his team on the power play and shut down opponents in his own end. Fans sometimes get nervous when he takes chances with the puck, but Subban is one of the most exciting young defensemen in the NHL.

SCOTT STEVENS

Hockey Hall of Fame: 2007

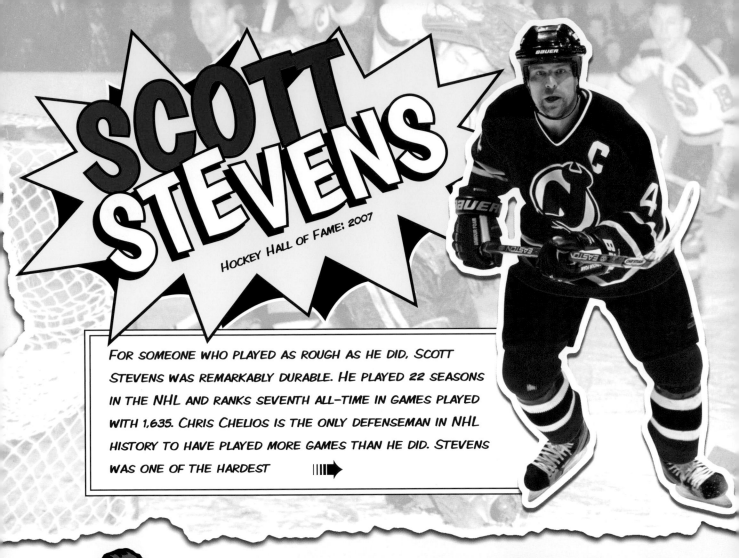

FOR SOMEONE WHO PLAYED AS ROUGH AS HE DID, SCOTT STEVENS WAS REMARKABLY DURABLE. HE PLAYED 22 SEASONS IN THE NHL AND RANKS SEVENTH ALL-TIME IN GAMES PLAYED WITH 1,635. CHRIS CHELIOS IS THE ONLY DEFENSEMAN IN NHL HISTORY TO HAVE PLAYED MORE GAMES THAN HE DID. STEVENS WAS ONE OF THE HARDEST ▐▐▐▶

SPRAGUE CLEGHORN (HHOF: 1958) — Blast from the Past

Sprague Cleghorn began his pro hockey career in 1910–11, seven years before the NHL was formed. He later starred in the NHL until 1927–28, often playing with his brother Odie. Sprague was one of the top-scoring defensemen of his era and is considered to be one of the toughest players of all-time. In fact, many oldtimers thought he was the dirtiest player they ever faced! Still, there was no denying that Cleghorn had talent. He won the Stanley Cup with Ottawa in 1920 and 1921 and was captain of the Montreal Canadiens when they won it in 1924.

hitters in hockey history. Sometimes, he was accused of playing dirty, but mostly he was admired for his tough, physical skill.

Stevens played just one full season of junior hockey. He was a teammate of future Hall of Famer Al MacInnis with the Kitchener Rangers in 1981–82 and helped that team win the Memorial Cup. Stevens was then selected fifth overall by the Washington Capitals in the 1982 NHL Draft and made the team right away. In Washington, Stevens played with two other future Hall of Fame defensemen: Rod Langway and Larry Murphy. During the first half of his career, Stevens picked up plenty of points. He scored a career-high 21 goals for Washington in 1984–85 and had 60-plus assists three times. In 1993–94 he had a career-best 78 points for the New Jersey Devils.

Over his years in New Jersey, Stevens

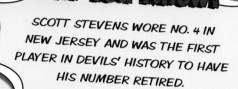

Did You Know?

SCOTT STEVENS WORE NO. 4 IN NEW JERSEY AND WAS THE FIRST PLAYER IN DEVILS' HISTORY TO HAVE HIS NUMBER RETIRED.

concentrated more on his hard-hitting defensive skills and the Devils became the NHL's toughest team to score against. He knew the Norris Trophy usually went to a defenseman with a lot of points, but he didn't mind that focusing on stopping scorers would limit his chances at winning the trophy. Stevens was captain of the Devils from 1992–93 until his final season of 2002–03 and he led the team to three Stanley Cup wins. Stevens never did win the Norris Trophy, but he won the Conn Smythe Trophy as playoff MVP in 2000.

DUSTIN BYFUGLIEN (pronounced "Bufflin") is built more like a football linebacker than a hockey player. Though he keeps his game pretty clean, just the sight of the 6-foot-5 (196 cm), 265-pound (120 kg) defenseman can be intimidating! Byfuglien played defense in junior hockey and joined the Chicago Blackhawks as a defenseman in 2005–06. In 2007–08, Chicago moved him to right wing to take advantage of his size in front of the other team's net. Byfuglien helped Chicago win the Stanley Cup in 2010. Then he was traded to the Winnipeg Jets, where once again he is an imposing force on the blue line.

MODERN MATCH

DUSTIN BYFUGLIEN

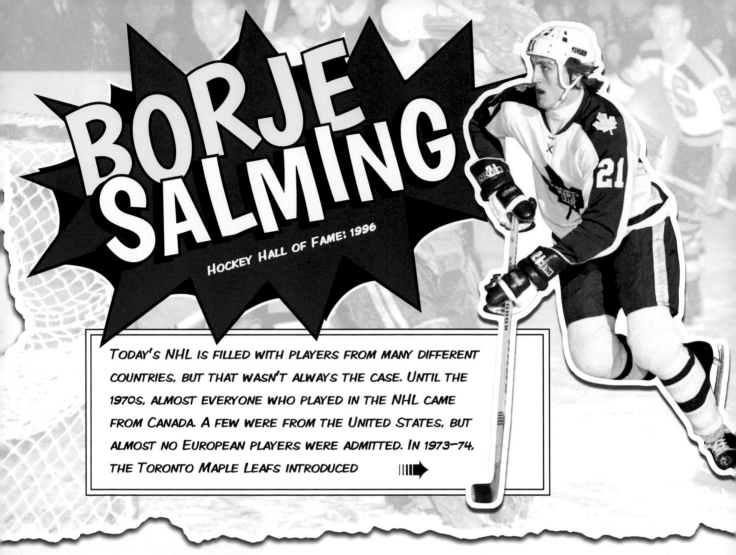

BORJE SALMING

Hockey Hall of Fame: 1996

TODAY'S NHL IS FILLED WITH PLAYERS FROM MANY DIFFERENT COUNTRIES, BUT THAT WASN'T ALWAYS THE CASE. UNTIL THE 1970s, ALMOST EVERYONE WHO PLAYED IN THE NHL CAME FROM CANADA. A FEW WERE FROM THE UNITED STATES, BUT ALMOST NO EUROPEAN PLAYERS WERE ADMITTED. IN 1973–74, THE TORONTO MAPLE LEAFS INTRODUCED ▶

DETROIT RED WINGS: 1991–92 TO 2011–12

Nicklas
LIDSTROM

THE EUROPEAN CONNECTION

Nicklas Lidstrom arrived in Detroit in 1991–92, just two years after Borje Salming ended his career with the Red Wings. Over the next 20 years, Lidstrom became one of the greatest defensemen in NHL history. He won the Norris Trophy seven times! Lidstrom posted plenty of points, and was an excellent defender that relied on his hockey smarts to keep opponents under control. Lidstrom was the NHL's first European-trained captain to lead his team to the Stanley Cup. He was also the first European-trained player to be named playoff MVP!

a 22-year-old defenseman from Sweden. Borje Salming was not the first European player to make it to the NHL, but he was the first to become a star. His success opened the door for every European player that has followed.

It was almost an accident that Salming made it to the NHL. The Maple Leafs were actually looking at another Swedish player when they noticed Salming. Toronto signed Salming and fellow Swede Inge Hammarstrom. There was not much body contact in Swedish hockey, and people wondered if Salming would be tough enough for the NHL. Players on other teams called him "chicken" and tried to scare him with rough play. Salming never let the bullies get him down and he soon earned everyone's respect.

Salming kept himself in great shape and often played more than half the game. He was a fearless shot-blocker, which was rare back then because protective gear was so much smaller than it is today. By his second season of 1974–75, he was comfortable enough in the NHL to unleash his offensive skill. He became known for his dazzling zigzag rushes and slick passes. He didn't have a big slap shot, but his wrist shot was dangerous. Salming finished his NHL career with the Detroit Red Wings in 1989–90, but remains one of the most popular Maple Leafs of all time. He never won the Norris Trophy as the NHL's best defenseman, but finished second in voting twice.

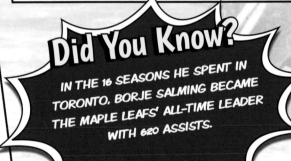

Did You Know?

IN THE 16 SEASONS HE SPENT IN TORONTO, BORJE SALMING BECAME THE MAPLE LEAFS' ALL-TIME LEADER WITH 620 ASSISTS.

LIKE SALMING, Erik Karlsson is a powerful skater who can fly across the ice. He's got a booming slap shot too! When he was only 17 years old, Karlsson had already reached the top league in Sweden. Later that year, Ottawa selected him in the first round of the 2008 NHL Draft. He joined the Senators in 2009–10. Karlsson led all NHL defensemen with 78 points in 2011–12 and won the Norris Trophy that season. He'd barely turned 22 when the award was announced, making him the youngest Norris Trophy winner since Bobby Orr in 1968.

MODERN MATCH
ERIK KARLSSON

RAYMOND BOURQUE

HOCKEY HALL OF FAME: 2004

RAYMOND BOURQUE BROKE INTO THE NHL IN 1979–80, THE SAME YEAR AS WAYNE GRETZKY. BOURQUE WAS THE WINNER OF THE CALDER TROPHY AS ROOKIE OF THE YEAR THAT SEASON. THE NHL DECIDED GRETZKY COULDN'T WIN THE AWARD BECAUSE HE PLAYED PROFESSIONALLY IN THE WORLD HOCKEY ASSOCIATION THE YEAR BEFORE. EVEN SO, BOURQUE ▐▐▐▶

RYAN SUTER IS part of a famous American hockey family. His father, Bob Suter, won a gold medal with the 1980 U.S. Olympic team. His uncle, Gary Suter, had a 17-year career in the NHL. Ryan began his NHL career with Nashville in 2005. He quickly became a star defenseman, but he got even better with Minnesota. With the Wild in 2012–13, Suter had more time on ice than any other player in the NHL. He was named the league's best defenseman by *The Hockey News* and finished second in voting for the Norris Trophy behind Montreal's P.K. Subban.

MODERN MATCH

RYAN SUTER

had an amazing season! His 65 points that year set a record for rookie defensemen. Not only did Bourque win the Calder Trophy, he was also named a First-Team All-Star. It was the first time in NHL history that anyone but a goalie had won both awards in one year. Bourque went on to earn 13 selections to the First All-Star Team during his 22-year career. That's the most by anyone who's ever played in the NHL!

Bourque played with a calm style that made things look easy. He was a smooth, effortless skater, and he

kept himself in excellent shape, which allowed him to get plenty of ice time. Even late in his career, Bourque often played more than 30 minutes per game! He had plenty of offensive skill, but he was truly a two-way talent. He could play a strong, physical game in his own end of the rink, and also make passes with great finesse to set up his teammates. Bourque reached a career high with 31 goals in 1983–84 and scored 20 goals or more eight other times. The only time he failed to score at least 10 goals was in his final NHL season, when he was 40 years old.

When Bourque retired in 2001, he'd become the all-time leader among NHL defensemen with 410 goals and 1,169 assists for 1,579 points. He'd also won the Norris Trophy five times.

Did You Know?

RAYMOND BOURQUE WAS CAPTAIN OF THE BOSTON BRUINS FOR A TEAM-RECORD 12 YEARS FROM 1988 TO 2000.

CUP-WINNING THREADS

Raymond Bourque played 20 full seasons for the Boston Bruins. He was one of the greatest players in the NHL, but he'd never won the Stanley Cup. Late in the 1999–2000 season, Bourque was traded to Colorado, one of the top teams in the NHL at that time. In 2000–01, the Avalanche plotted mission 16W — 16 wins being the amount of playoff victories a team needed to claim the Stanley Cup. When they completed the mission, Bourque was the first player to raise the Cup over his head. Bourque wore this jersey during the second period of Game 7 in the 2001 Stanley Cup Final.

FROM THE VAULT

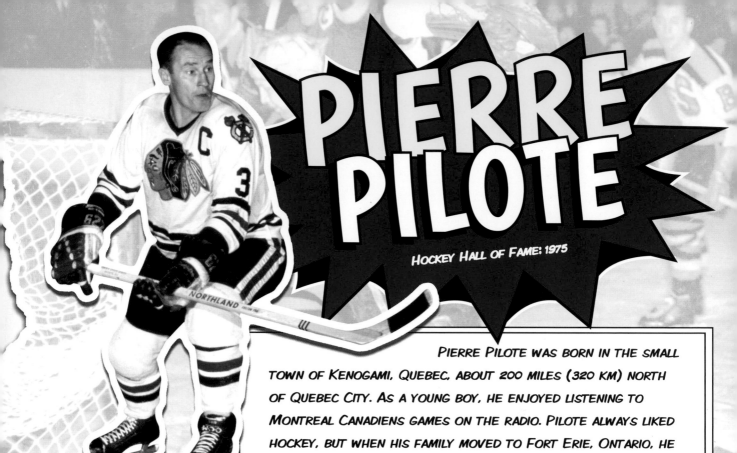

PIERRE PILOTE

HOCKEY HALL OF FAME: 1975

PIERRE PILOTE WAS BORN IN THE SMALL TOWN OF KENOGAMI, QUEBEC, ABOUT 200 MILES (320 KM) NORTH OF QUEBEC CITY. AS A YOUNG BOY, HE ENJOYED LISTENING TO MONTREAL CANADIENS GAMES ON THE RADIO. PILOTE ALWAYS LIKED HOCKEY, BUT WHEN HIS FAMILY MOVED TO FORT ERIE, ONTARIO, HE FELL IN LOVE WITH BASEBALL HE PLAYED ON TWO ▐▐▐▶

JACK STEWART (HHOF: 1964) — Blast FROM THE Past

Jack Stewart was known as the hardest hitting defenseman of his era. Opponents often said he got a big smile on his face when he was about to give a check. Like Pilote, he was rough, and sometimes took a lot of penalties, but most of his hits were clean. Stewart joined the Red Wings in 1938–39 and helped Detroit win the Stanley Cup in 1942–43 and 1949–50. He was traded to Chicago before the 1950–51 season and was immediately named team captain. Stewart suffered two serious injuries while playing in Chicago and retired from the NHL in 1952.

All-Ontario champions and dreamed of making the Majors. Pilote was 16 before he started playing hockey seriously. Soon, he was good enough that NHL teams were interested in him.

Pilote began playing junior hockey in St. Catharines, near his home in Fort Erie, in 1950. In 1952, he turned pro with the Buffalo Bisons of the American Hockey League. Then, in 1955, the Black Hawks bought the Bisons and made the club their farm team; with the purchase, Chicago was given the rights to the Bisons' players. Before long, Pilote was playing with the Black Hawks. Chicago was the worst team in the league back then, but soon, other players arrived from the farm system. With Pilote, Bobby Hull, Stan Mikita and others, things quickly got better in Chicago.

Pilote was aggressive and often difficult to deal with. When he was younger he

Did You Know?

PIERRE PILOTE EARNED EIGHT STRAIGHT SELECTIONS AS A FIRST- OR SECOND-TEAM ALL-STAR FROM 1959–60 TO 1966–67.

would lose his temper and take bad penalties. He became more effective when he learned to control his temper, and his strong play helped Chicago win the Stanley Cup in 1960–61. The next season Pilote was named captain! Pilote was always a strong checker in his own end, but he was also very good at passing the puck. His all-around play was rewarded in 1962–63 when he won the Norris Trophy for the first of three straight seasons. In 1964–65, Pilote had 14 goals and 45 assists for 59 points, which set a new record for defensemen at that time.

AT 6-FOOT-3 (190 cm) and 221 pounds (100 kg), Brent Seabrook has a great combination of size, strength and speed. He's solid in his own end and often gets a lot of ice time against the other team's best forwards. Seabrook also has a hard shot from the blue line and is good at passing the puck. Chicago picked Seabrook 14th overall in the 2003 NHL Draft. He joined the Blackhawks in 2005–06 and helped them win the Stanley Cup in 2010.

Seabrook scored two big overtime goals during the 2013 playoffs to help Chicago win the Cup again.

MODERN MATCH
BRENT SEABROOK

BRAD PARK

HOCKEY HALL OF FAME: 1988

It was Brad Park's bad luck that his career overlapped Bobby Orr's best years. Many people think Orr is the greatest defenseman in hockey history. Park always seemed to be runner-up; in fact, he never won the Norris Trophy as the league's best defenseman, but was second in voting six times! Like Orr, Park was a strong ▮▮▮▶

Blast FROM THE Past

CHING JOHNSON (HHOF: 1958)

Ching Johnson joined the New York Rangers when they entered the NHL in 1926–27. At 5-foot-11 (180 cm) and 210 pounds (95 kg), he was huge for his era and was one of the game's hardest checkers. His defense partner, Clarence "Taffy" Abel, was even bigger, at 6-foot-1 (185 cm) and 225 pounds (103 kg). It was tough for any forward to get past those two! There was no Norris Trophy back then, but in the first four years that the NHL chose All-Stars, Johnson earned two selections to the First Team and two to the Second.

skater who loved to rush the puck. He was also a smart playmaker with a hard, accurate shot. Defensively, Park would steer opponents away from the middle of the ice and toward the boards. Even when a player seemed to beat him, that player was usually in poor position for a shot on goal.

When Park was playing minor hockey in Toronto, people worried that he was too small to make the NHL. It's true that Park was barely 5-feet tall (152 cm) when he was 15 years old, but he later shot up to 6-feet (183 cm) and 200 pounds (91 kg). In 1966, the New York Rangers made him the second pick in the NHL Draft. When he joined the team in 1968–69, Park finished third in voting for the rookie of the year. In 1969–70, he finished second to Orr for the Norris Trophy and joined the great Boston Bruins blueliner as a First-Team

Did You Know?

WHEN HE RETIRED IN 1985, BRAD PARK'S 683 CAREER ASSISTS WERE THE MOST EVER BY AN NHL DEFENSEMAN.

All-Star. At 21 years old, Park was the youngest Ranger ever to earn that honor. In 1972, he helped the Rangers reach the Stanley Cup final.

Park was named captain of the Rangers in 1974, but early in the 1975–76 season he was traded to Boston. Knee injuries had practically ended Bobby Orr's career and Park replaced him on the Bruins blue line. Park helped the Bruins reach the finals in 1977 and 1978, but he never won the Stanley Cup.

MODERN MATCH DREW DOUGHTY

THE LOS ANGELES KINGS chose Drew Doughty second overall at the 2008 NHL Draft. Though he'd been a star in junior hockey with the Guelph Storm, Doughty knew it would be tough to make the Kings as an 18-year-old. He worked hard at training camp and earned a spot. Doughty made the NHL All-Rookie Team in 2008–09 and was even better in 2009–10. He won an Olympic gold medal and finished third in voting for the Norris Trophy. Doughty won a second Olympic gold in 2014. Like Park, Doughty loves to skate with the puck and has the stamina to log a ton of ice time.

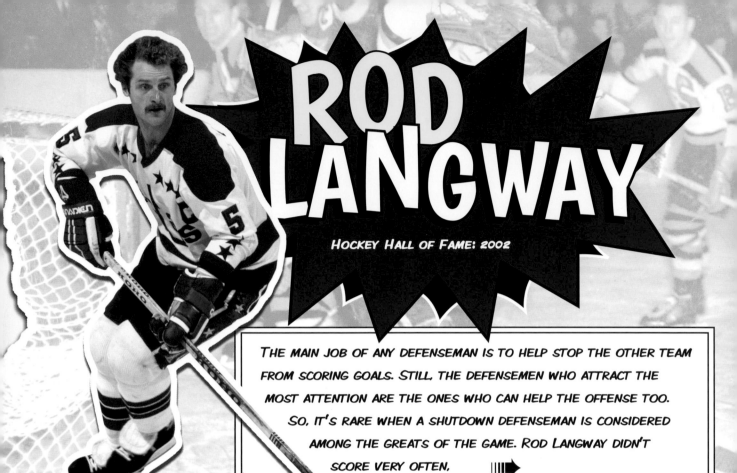

ROD LANGWAY

Hockey Hall of Fame: 2002

The main job of any defenseman is to help stop the other team from scoring goals. Still, the defensemen who attract the most attention are the ones who can help the offense too. So, it's rare when a shutdown defenseman is considered among the greats of the game. Rod Langway didn't score very often, ▐▐▐▶

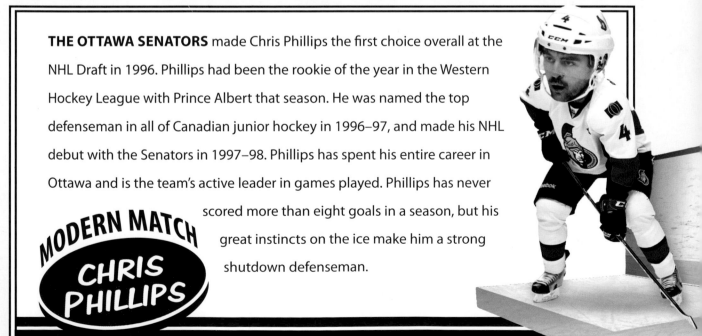

MODERN MATCH: CHRIS PHILLIPS

THE OTTAWA SENATORS made Chris Phillips the first choice overall at the NHL Draft in 1996. Phillips had been the rookie of the year in the Western Hockey League with Prince Albert that season. He was named the top defenseman in all of Canadian junior hockey in 1996–97, and made his NHL debut with the Senators in 1997–98. Phillips has spent his entire career in Ottawa and is the team's active leader in games played. Phillips has never scored more than eight goals in a season, but his great instincts on the ice make him a strong shutdown defenseman.

but he was too good at shutting down opponents to be ignored. Langway scored just three goals for the Washington Capitals in 1982–83, and yet he won the Norris Trophy. No other winner of the NHL's award for best defenseman has ever scored fewer goals! Langway won the Norris Trophy again in 1983–84. He had nine goals that year. Wayne Gretzky had 87 goals, 118 assists and 205 points that season and yet Langway finished second to "The Great One" in voting as NHL MVP.

Langway was born in Taipei, Taiwan, where his father served in the United States Navy. He grew up in Randolph, Massachusetts, near Boston. Langway played football and baseball as a boy, and didn't begin to play organized hockey until he was 13. Football was his best sport, but he loved hockey too. Many American universities wanted him to play football, but Langway chose the University of New Hampshire because

they let him play both sports. In 1977, the Montreal Canadiens picked Langway in the second round of the NHL Draft. He joined the team in 1978–79 and helped Montreal win the Stanley Cup for the fourth year in a row that season.

Langway was traded to Washington in 1982 and named captain of the team. The Capitals, who had never made the playoffs before Langway's arrival, never missed the postseason during his 11 years with the team!

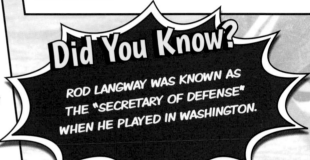

Did You Know?

ROD LANGWAY WAS KNOWN AS THE "SECRETARY OF DEFENSE" WHEN HE PLAYED IN WASHINGTON.

Blast FROM THE Past   BUTCH BOUCHARD

Growing up during The Great Depression, Butch Bouchard couldn't afford to buy skates. He didn't even learn to skate until he was 16, but Bouchard was a great athlete and took to hockey quickly. In 1941, he rode his bicycle 35 miles (50 km) to go to training camp with the Montreal Canadiens! He made the team, and played with them for 15 years. Bouchard helped Montreal win the Stanley Cup four times and was captain of the team from 1948 to 1956. His strong play in his own end allowed defense partner Doug Harvey the freedom to rush with the puck.

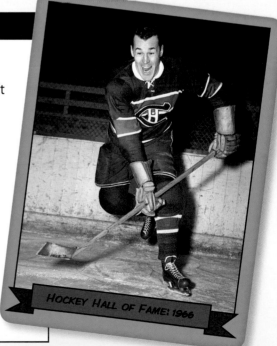

HOCKEY HALL OF FAME: 1966

CHRIS CHELIOS

Hockey Hall of Fame: 2013

CHRIS CHELIOS IS A DINOSAUR! WELL, NOT REALLY, BUT BY THE TIME HE RETIRED NO DEFENSEMAN IN NHL HISTORY HAD A LONGER CAREER THAN HIM. HE PLAYED HIS LAST NHL GAME WHEN HE WAS 48 YEARS OLD! HE RANKS FIFTH ALL-TIME IN GAMES PLAYED IN THE REGULAR SEASON WITH 1,651. ONLY GORDIE HOWE CAN MATCH THE 26 SEASONS CHELIOS SPENT IN THE NHL. |||▶

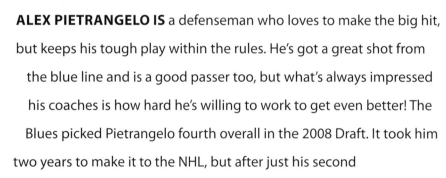

ALEX PIETRANGELO IS a defenseman who loves to make the big hit, but keeps his tough play within the rules. He's got a great shot from the blue line and is a good passer too, but what's always impressed his coaches is how hard he's willing to work to get even better! The Blues picked Pietrangelo fourth overall in the 2008 Draft. It took him two years to make it to the NHL, but after just his second full season with the Blues in 2011–12, he was named a Second-Team All-Star. In 2014 he won a gold medal with the Canadian Olympic team!

MODERN MATCH
ALEX PIETRANGELO

Chelios learned to play hockey in his hometown of Chicago, but it looked like he might have to stop playing when he was 15 and his family moved to California. There were no local teams to play on. Finally, when he was 17, Chelios ventured to Canada and joined the Moose Jaw Canucks in Saskatchewan. He was moved from forward to defense and was good enough that the Montreal Canadiens took him in the second round of the 1981 Draft. In his first full season with the Canadiens in 1984–85, Chelios finished second in voting behind Mario Lemieux for rookie of the year. The next season, he helped the Canadiens win the Stanley Cup. Soon, Chelios was one of the best defensemen in the NHL. He won his first Norris Trophy in 1988–89.

Chelios was traded to Chicago in 1990 and won the Norris Trophy twice with the

Blackhawks. He was captain of the team from 1995 until 1999 when he was traded to Detroit. He helped the Red Wings win the Stanley Cup in 2002 and 2008. Chelios never looked fancy on the ice, but he was strong and tough. He was a good offensive defenseman, but it was his hard hits and all-out effort that made him so great. Chelios' secret to playing for so many years was to keep himself in peak physical shape. His workouts even included surfing!

Blast FROM THE Past   RED HORNER (HHOF: 1965)

Like Chelios, Red Horner was never graceful on the ice, but he could always deliver a hard hit. He was a solid defenseman who starred for 12 seasons with the Toronto Maple Leafs from 1928 to 1940. For much of that time, Horner was known as the "Bad Boy of Hockey." He led the NHL in penalty minutes eight seasons in a row. But Horner was no mere goon. He helped the Leafs finish first in their division four times and he won the Stanley Cup with Toronto in 1932. He was also captain of the Leafs from 1938 to 1940.

RED KELLY

HOCKEY HALL OF FAME: 1969

LEONARD "RED" KELLY HAD ONE BRILLIANT NHL CAREER DIVIDED INTO TWO VERY DISTINCT HALVES: FOR MORE THAN 12 YEARS WITH THE DETROIT RED WINGS, KELLY WAS ONE OF HOCKEY'S BEST DEFENSEMEN. THEN, FOR NEARLY EIGHT YEARS WITH THE TORONTO MAPLE LEAFS, HE WAS ONE OF THE GAME'S BEST CENTERS. IN ALL, KELLY WON THE STANLEY CUP EIGHT TIMES: ▐▐▐▶

DIT CLAPPER (HHOF: 1947)

Blast FROM THE Past

Like Kelly, Dit Clapper split his time between forward and defense. He was the first person to play 20 seasons in the NHL, and he spent his entire career in Boston. Clapper played right wing when he joined the Bruins in 1927–28. He helped them win the Stanley Cup in 1929 and soon became one of the NHL's top scorers. After 10 seasons at right wing, Boston moved Clapper to defense in 1937–38. A year later, he helped the Bruins win the Stanley Cup again! Clapper was an All-Star twice at right wing and four times as a defenseman.

four times with Detroit and four times with Toronto! His eight Stanley Cup wins are the most ever for someone who never played for the Montreal Canadiens — and they won a lot of Stanley Cups!

Kelly grew up in the small town of Simcoe, Ontario and he cheered for the Maple Leafs. His favorite player was Toronto defenseman Red Horner, who (like Kelly) was nicknamed for his hair color. Horner, however, was one of the roughest players in NHL history, and when Kelly made the NHL he played a completely different style. Kelly

won the Lady Byng Trophy for sportsmanship four times, which is a rare feat for a defenseman because stopping offensive players often means using rough play, and that leads to penalties. After Kelly won the Byng in 1953–54, it took almost 60 years for another defenseman to win it!

Kelly had hoped to play with the Maple Leafs, but it was the Red Wings that invited him to training camp. He made the team right away in 1947 and built a reputation for playing clean yet strong hockey. He was an effective checker, and his solid skating and puck-moving skills helped Detroit on offense. With other stars such as Gordie Howe, Ted Lindsay and Terry Sawchuk, Detroit quickly became the top team in the NHL. From 1948–49 to 1954–55, the Red Wings finished first in the regular-season standings a record seven years in a row!

Did You Know?

RED KELLY WAS THE WINNER OF THE NORRIS TROPHY THE FIRST TIME IT WAS PRESENTED, BACK IN 1953–54.

VICTORY GARB

Red Kelly wore this jersey for Toronto throughout the 1966–67 season. There were only six teams in the NHL back then. The Chicago Black Hawks were the best team in the NHL that season, but the Maple Leafs shocked them in the opening round of the playoffs. Then, in the finals, Toronto beat Montreal in six games to win the Stanley Cup! Kelly was one of several veterans with Toronto that season. Even though he was 39 years old, the Maple Leafs offered him a new, four-year contract, but Kelly decided to retire while he was on top.

FROM THE VAULT

TORONTO MAPLE LEAFS

VIACHESLAV FETISOV

Hockey Hall of Fame: 2001

EVEN THOUGH HE NEVER PLAYED IN THE NHL, VIACHESLAV FETISOV IS WIDELY CONSIDERED ONE OF THE GREATEST DEFENSEMEN EVER. "SLAVA," AS HE WAS KNOWN, WAS A BIG AND STRONG DEFENDER WHO WAS ALSO FAST ON HIS FEET. HE COULD SHUT DOWN TOP FORWARDS, AND HE HAD A KNACK FOR KNOWING WHEN TO PINCH IN FROM THE BLUE LINE TO CREATE SCORING CHANCES. ▶

WHEN SERGEI GONCHAR reached the top league in Russia in 1991, it was becoming common for Russians to play in the NHL. He was drafted by Washington in 1992 and joined the Capitals two years later. In 1998–99, he scored 21 times to become the first Russian defenseman to top the 20-goal plateau. He had a career-high 26 goals in 2001–02. Gonchar has gone on to play for Boston, Pittsburgh, Ottawa and Dallas. When Evgeni Malkin joined the Penguins in 2006–07, he lived with Gonchar for a while. Together, they helped the Penguins win the Stanley Cup in 2009.

MODERN MATCH

SERGEI GONCHAR

Fetisov was born in Russia, and he joined Moscow's Central Red Army junior team as a 16-year-old in 1974–75. In 1977 and 1978, he helped the Soviet Union (Russia) win the first two official World Junior Championships. He was named the Best Defenseman at the tournament in 1978 and was selected to the All-Star Team along with another future superstar, Wayne Gretzky. Fetisov was just 19 years old in 1978, but he played alongside grown men in the World Championships that year too. Remarkably, he was named the Best Defenseman at the Worlds. It was the first of six times he'd win that honor, and the first of seven times he'd help the Soviets win the World title! Fetisov made his first appearance at the Olympics in 1980. The United States won a surprising gold medal that year, with the Soviets taking silver. Fetisov later won

Olympic gold medals in 1984 and 1988. He also won the Golden Stick Award as the best player in Europe three times!

For many years, players from the Soviet Union were not allowed to leave Russia to join the NHL, but that changed, and in 1989 Fetisov finally got his chance. He was 31 years old when he joined the New Jersey Devils. He was traded to Detroit in 1995 where he was one of five Russian players that helped the Red Wings win the Stanley Cup in 1997 and 1998.

FROM RIVAL TO TEAMMATE

Larry Murphy's NHL career began with a bang when he recorded 76 points for Los Angeles in 1980–81. That's a rookie record for defensemen that still stands. Murphy went on to play 21 years in the NHL and ranks fifth all-time among defensemen with 1,216 points. In 1987, Murphy was a member of Team Canada when they defeated Slava Fetisov and the Soviet Union in a thrilling Canada Cup championship. Many people consider that to be the greatest tournament in hockey history. Ten years later, Murphy joined Fetisov in Detroit and helped the Red Wings win back-to-back Stanley Cups.

HOCKEY HALL OF FAME: 2004

Larry MURPHY

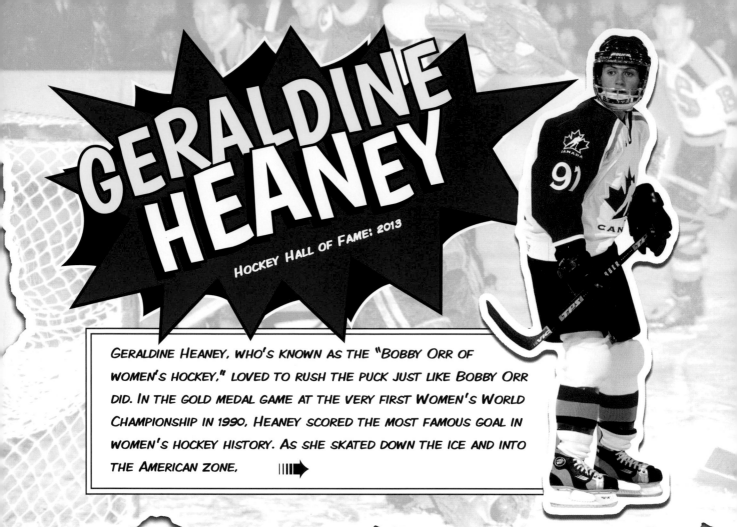

GERALDINE HEANEY

Hockey Hall of Fame: 2013

GERALDINE HEANEY, WHO'S KNOWN AS THE "BOBBY ORR OF WOMEN'S HOCKEY," LOVED TO RUSH THE PUCK JUST LIKE BOBBY ORR DID. IN THE GOLD MEDAL GAME AT THE VERY FIRST WOMEN'S WORLD CHAMPIONSHIP IN 1990, HEANEY SCORED THE MOST FAMOUS GOAL IN WOMEN'S HOCKEY HISTORY. AS SHE SKATED DOWN THE ICE AND INTO THE AMERICAN ZONE, ▐▐▐➡

FROM THE VAULT

GOAL-SCORER'S DUDS

Geraldine Heaney wore this jersey with the Toronto Aeros in the National Women's Hockey League in 2003–04. It was Heaney's final season as a player and she ended the year in style. At the Esso Women's Nationals in March of 2004, the Aeros represented their home province as Team Ontario. In the championship game against Hayley Wickenheiser and Team Alberta, Heaney rushed end-to-end to score the winning goal for the Aeros at 3:39 of overtime. Making the play even more remarkable, Heaney was three months pregnant with her daughter Shannon at the time!

she split the U.S. defense and then lifted the puck over the goalie just before being knocked flying through the air. The goal gave Canada a 3–2 lead and sparked them to a 5–2 victory. Her goal was a lot like a goal scored by Bobby Orr to win the Stanley Cup in 1970. His is one of the most famous goals ever, and just like Heaney, Orr went flying through the air after he scored. Heaney's goal inspired many girls to play hockey, including future Team Canada star Cassie Campbell-Pascal. "When you're talking offensive defensemen in women's hockey," she once said, "Heaney's name will always be the one that comes up first."

Heaney was born in Northern Ireland, but she grew up in Toronto. When she was 13 years old in 1980, she began playing with the Toronto Aeros and she helped the team win six provincial championships over 18 seasons in the Ontario Women's Hockey Association. During that time Heaney was named the Most Valuable Defenseman three times!

Heaney represented Canada at the first seven Women's World Championships. She was the only Canadian player to appear in every one of those tournaments, and she helped Canada win a gold medal every time! The United States beat Canada at the first Winter Olympic tournament in 1998, but Heaney was back in 2002 to help Canada win Olympic gold that year in her last international event!

Did You Know?

GERALDINE HEANEY WAS THE ONLY PERSON TO PLAY IN EVERY CANADIAN WOMEN'S NATIONAL CHAMPIONSHIP FROM 1987 TO 2001.

Dynamite Teammates

ANGELA JAMES (HHOF: 2010)

In 2010, American Cammi Granato and Canadian Angela James were the first women to be inducted into the Hockey Hall of Fame. Like Geraldine Heaney, James grew up in Toronto. There were so few girls' hockey teams when she was young that James played with boys. When she got older, she led the Ontario Women's Hockey Association in scoring eight times! She also won six league MVP awards. During the 1990s, James and Heaney were teammates with the Toronto Aeros and with the Canadian national team.

INDEX

PHOTO CREDITS

T=Top, B= Bottom, BL=Bottom left, BR=Bottom right

All illustrations © George Todorovic

Hockey Hall of Fame

Graphic Artists/HHOF 6T, 20 BL, 20BR, 22T, 28T, 32T, 34T; Paul Bereswill/HHOF 42T; Hockey Hall of Fame 16T; Doug MacLellan/HHOF 7B, 14T; Matthew Manor/HHOF 11B, 17B, 44T, 45B; O-Pee-Chee/HHOF 5 (Langway), 36T; Portnoy/HHOF 12T, 20T; Chris Relke/HHOF 8T; Hal Roth/HHOF 24B, 31B, 41B, 44B; Dave Sandford/HHOF 5 (Niedermayer, Bourque, Stevens), 10T, 14B, 18T, 26T, 28B, 30T, 38T, 43B; Imperial Oil–Turofsky/HHOF 5 (Harvey), 24T, 37B, 40T.

All images used for the cover are listed above as they appear in the book.

Icon Sports Images

Chris Austin/Icon SMI 19B; Dustin Bradford/Icon SMI 42B; Matt Cohen/Icon SMI 29B; Rich Graessle/Icon SMI 33B; Rich Kane/Icon SMI 10B; Fred Kfoury/Icon SMI 5 (Chara), 16B, 36B; Jeanine Leech/Icon SMI 5 (Subban), 12B, 21B, 25B; Mark LoMoglio/Icon SMI 15B; Brad Rempel/Icon SMI 30B; Juan Salas/Icon SMI 27B; Ric Tapia/Icon SMI 38B; Michael Tureski/Icon SMI 22B; Chris Williams/Icon SMI 5 (Doughty), 35B; Warren Wimmer/Icon SMI 9B.